Succeeding

with

Schizophrenia

Succeeding *with* Schizophrenia

Authors

Dr. Austin A. Mardon

Dr. Catherine Mardon

Jonathan Wiebe

David Supina

Zach Irving

Yash Bhatia

GM PRESS

First Printing: 2022

Cover Design and typeset by Clare Dalton

ISBN 978-1-77369-774-1

E-book ISBN 978-1-77369-775-8

Golden Meteorite Press

103 11919 82 St NW

Edmonton, AB T5B 2W3

www.goldenmeteoritepress.com

Foreword

A great deal of time has been spent trying to understand various illnesses; people have worked to determine their ins and outs, their pathology, their symptoms, their cures or treatments - but one thing that seems to often be forgotten in these explorations is how to live with them. Or, better yet, make the most of them. Now, not every illness is going to last the rest of your life. Many won't even leave signs that they were ever there once gone. But if you or someone close to you has been diagnosed with schizophrenia, then things are going to be different, and odds are they're never going to be the same. With as far as we've come with our treatments and medications, schizophrenia is absolutely a manageable condition, but the life you're going to have with it won't be the one you hoped for or dreamed about growing up.

As dreary a start as that is, something that everybody working on this book hopes you take away, above all else, is that there is still hope. Dr. Austin Mardon - someone you will be reading a lot about over the course of this book - more than anything else, considers his life with schizophrenia to be a story of hope. Through all the many ups and downs, of everything he accomplished before and after schizophrenia, what he has said interview after interview and book after book, is that there is still hope. That if he can do it, then anyone can - so long as you don't give up.

Though this isn't the only book out there on living with schizophrenia - or even the only book on it written with and about Austin Mardon - our goal with this book is to go past what is normally covered. Rather than just share with you tips and tricks about how to survive and get through life with schizophrenia, with this book we wanted to share with you information on how to succeed with it. Though life with schizophrenia likely isn't what anybody had planned for or expected, and a lot is going to change, there is no reason it has to be the end of your life. Through this book, we hope to show you that instead, it can be a new beginning.

So that's this book in a slightly long-winded nutshell: Austin's life story of hope, perseverance, and success. We hope that through this book, and through Dr. Mardon's story and advice, you are able to find some of the hope and strength of will that led Austin to defy expectations, and make his own, simply incredible success.

And remember, when everyone is telling you that your life is over, success is survival and having meaning in your life. So don't give up, because, as Austin often says, "there is hope."

A Day in Austin's Life

To start this book, we are going to take a look at what the average day for Dr. Austin Mardon looks like. However, this exploration of Dr. Mardon's life is not to tell you what your life with schizophrenia or with someone with schizophrenia will look like - his life is not meant to be taken as a prediction or to be perfectly generalizable to all schizophrenics. Dr. Mardon is a particularly unique person - more unique than most even without considering his illness - and the exploration of his daily life and overall focus on him throughout the book is not meant to present him as 'average,' 'typical,' or even necessarily representative of all you or your loved ones will see and experience. What this exploration, and later explorations of Dr. Mardon and his life are meant to do though, is to show you some of the realities of life with schizophrenia, some of the limitations and downsides of it, as well as that, while life will be different, happiness and fulfillment are still entirely within reach - just maybe not in the way you planned or expected. With a life as full as Austin's, you end up with a lot to offer and teach, and when it comes to not just surviving but succeeding with schizophrenia, I doubt there's anyone who will be able to teach more than him.

Dr. Mardon starts his average day early, waking up around 7 to 8 AM, and begins with breakfast and calmly going through emails for around a half hour. With everything Austin manages to fit into his days - all the various projects, students, people of interest who he's hounding to make changes or to contribute to one thing or another - he gets a lot of emails. From there, he spends 2-3 hours dealing with what he referred to as "disability issues:" handling his medications, various trips or calls to and from doctors' offices, paperwork - those kinds of things. For Austin, the paperwork alone that he fills out is almost like a full-time job, and while the paperwork is not always the same and does include things for others like his wife Catherine, or their adoptive and foster children, or any number of his projects or endeavours, there is still more than enough concerning his illness and everything to do with it. It was at this point in my interview with Austin that he shared the "fun" fact about how he had to fill out close to 1000 pages of forms for veterans' benefits. Mind you, he applied for something like 25 consecutive claims, but even split evenly amongst each it is a lot of paperwork. After these couple of hours of paperwork, Dr. Mardon spends about a half hour every couple of days dealing with refills for his medications and any concerns or events that come up with them, such as lack of meds or confusion around prescriptions or payments. By the end of all this, usually around 11:30 AM, Austin's morning will be done, and he'll have lunch with Catherine. From here he'll spend time with her, talking to her as well as students as need be, and taking a break. However, following this it's back to business, as Austin normally spends the next few hours until 3:30 to 4 doing more disability paperwork, taking him just about to the evening, when he spends time with his family - in between handling whatever emails or phone calls come his way.

While perhaps not what many would consider the most thrilling of days, Austin made the comment that his days are never the same, and he never gets bored - even though some elements and the general themes of his days remain relatively constant in his routine. Of course, beyond the need to be proactive with his and his family's paperwork in order to ensure everything continues running smoothly and gets done, and to keep all the various organizations and groups receiving all that paperwork separate in his head, Austin does have plenty more to keep him busy. In addition to his regular handling of medications and doctors,

Austin tries to call his doctor every couple of days, because of how stressful dealing with all the paperwork can be. Plus, though currently he and Catherine are not able to go out together much, normally they would, and Austin still tries to go out for coffee when he can get a ride somewhere. And of course, his non-profit organization - the Antarctic Institute of Canada (AIC) - and its various works and machinations fill in plenty of the time in between, as he manages any number of books, articles, board games and more being worked on at the same time. By working through and with various programs and groups for funding, Austin is able to use the AIC to employ and empower students, giving them the chance to work together to research and plan and create works across mediums with the purpose of educating, raising awareness about issues, and combating stigma and misconceptions. Even with the amount he delegates - which he does a lot since, as he was quick to point out during our interview, he is disabled - sorting out funding and the management of all the groups and projects is more than enough to keep him occupied. But he does it, along with all his paperwork and various elements of daily and weekly personal management. He does it with the support of those close to him, through the empowerment of students, and through some sort of insurmountable stubbornness that leads him to refuse to do anything less when he has it in his power to do more.

Despite how much he does, all in all his routine - like most aspects of Dr. Mardon's life - is surprising, not to mention largely unassuming. If you were to look at a list of all of Austin's various accolades and accomplishments (spoiler, there is a lot of them), at first glance there would probably be quite the disconnect from what you see there and what you imagine when you read that first paragraph about Austin's average day to day life. When you think of someone who has published hundreds of books and articles, received over 25 medals and accommodations including the Order of St. Sylvester and the Order of Canada, and who has been to Antarctica and met the pope twice (more on those later), your first thought probably is not an unassuming man who lives humbly and spends large swathes of his days doing paperwork for his and his family's various disabilities. Of course, as you will see more clearly throughout most of the rest of this book, defying expectations is kind of just par for the course for Austin at this point.

Austin's day to day life is almost certainly not what most people aim or plan for - Austin's life certainly isn't anywhere close to the life of academia and education Austin had planned and expected for himself when he was younger - but how are you supposed to plan to be diagnosed with schizophrenia? When talking to Austin about the idea for this book, he wanted it to be something positive, something hopeful. After all, despite the many ups and downs of Austin's life and how much his diagnosis pulled out the rug from under his feet, Austin always says his life story is one of hope. That being said, Austin will be the first to tell you much schizophrenia and living with it can suck. It is certainly not some sort of 'blessing in disguise' - though Austin does hold that some of the changes in his life that came from it were - and it is not going to be easy or particularly fun, especially upon first being diagnosed. But if there's one thing that you can take away from this book, just one part of all the information and advice and lived experience that fills this book, it should be that there is hope. Austin's life may not be one that is planned for, or one that everyone would consider 'normal,' but it is a good and fulfilling one. It is a full life, a busy one, and one filled with purpose, and though not what he expected when growing up, one that Austin is more than happy with.

Of course, as was mentioned at the beginning of the chapter, there is no reason to expect your life to be exactly the same as Austin's from this point on. Though you or a loved one may share the same illness as Austin, this doesn't change the fact that you are still a unique person, and much more than your illness. Your life will be different, and going forward there will likely be a number of similarities with Austin's day to day life and the experiences he had post-diagnosis - particularly regarding the paperwork, because as Austin assured me there is quite a lot of it even when you're only handling your own - but your life is still very much your own. Plus, beyond how just normally speaking there is no reason to expect your life to be the same as someone you share one thing with - even when that one thing is something as big as schizophrenia - as we will soon see in far greater detail, Dr. Austin Mardon is no typical 'case' or person, and he hasn't really ever been. So going forward keep in mind that, yeah, this is going to suck. You're going to lose a lot, and depending on a number of factors, you may even have to restart from the ground up like Austin. But your life is far from over, and at the end of the day you're still going to be you. So don't give up; for all you know you'll be the next Dr. Austin Mardon or Dr. John Nash - who Austin likes to point out was both 'crazier' than him as well as more successful - or, just as well, simply another person who defied the expectations and stigmas, and carried on to live a happy life. In case you're still worried though, or incredulous at the thought that your life could ever be anything close to happy or normal again, let's take a look at the various ups and downs of Austin's incredible - and incredibly atypical - life up to this point.

The Story of Austin Mardon

When Dr. Austin Mardon was first diagnosed with schizophrenia at the age of 30 in 1992, he thought his life was over. More than that, for some time he felt as if it had actually ended - as if he had died,and was simply there existing. Many of the people around him thought and acted similarly, with some going so far as to mourn him, acting as though what he felt truly had occurred, and that the Austin they knew was dead and gone. As hard as it may be to believe though with a start like this, overall the life story you're about to read is far closer to a happy one than a sad one. Don't get me wrong - there are definitely some low points, the one that is probably of greatest note being the just mentioned point in Austin's life when he was diagnosed with schizophrenia, and he had to figure out how to carry on and start over with this new reality. But it's been far from all lows, as you could have hopefully guessed from the discussion of the previous chapter. Of course, as mentioned in the first line, Austin's diagnosis happened at what is currently just shy of the halfway point of his life, and while it is certainly a key point in his story, Austin's is a story best worth telling from the start.

As is the case for most people past the age of 25, Austin's life story is one that would take more than just a chapter or two to tell in its entirety - a fact that could probably be assumed considering how there are books published on specific periods of his life alone. As such, though every effort will be made to include the key moments and aspects of Austin's life, this will ultimately be an abridged version of his story, from the start to the present day. Austin Mardon was born in Edmonton, Alberta in June of 1962, and spent most of his youth in Lethbridge, Alberta. Austin's first exposure to schizophrenia was only a few years into his life and over two decades before his own diagnosis, when his mother, May, was diagnosed. Though attitudes and practices regarding mental illnesses have improved quite a lot since the 60s, and were far better during the 60s than for quite some time before, there was an incredible amount of stigma and fear surrounding his mother's diagnosis. With the way things were at the time, it was a difficult reality for his family to accept, and one that his mother never truly did. Despite this though, Austin's family life was fairly stable for most of his early years. Though Austin was bullied and shunned at school by his peers for being different, Austin did well, and got a passion for learning and life from his father, Ernest, who was a professor at the University of Lethbridge. It was also during this time in his life that Austin first became interested in the Antarctic and becoming an explorer. Shortly after though, things changed quite dramatically for Austin; in 1978, Austin's mother had a serious mental breakdown, and in order to avoid having their children taken away from them, Austin's father sent them to live at Ardross Castle in Scotland.

Austin's grandfather purchased the castle during the great depression, and in 1978 when Austin and his sisters were sent to live there, it was being taken care of by his aunt Lucy. Though a difficult transition at first, Austin grew close to his aunt during the time there, and ended up enjoying quite a lot of his time at the castle. He even had a better time at school, now being the mysterious new kid, and was able to go into it with a clean slate and no prior judgement. However, his and his sisters' stay at Ardross castle was only ever meant to be temporary, and before long Austin was on his way back home. Things didn't improve very much at school, actually getting worse academically as the courses he took in Scotland didn't line up with the Alberta curriculum, and the family dynamic stayed strange and strained. But life carried on, and at the age of 17 Austin applied to the University of Lethbridge hoping to start a new chapter of his life and pursue his interests. Unfortunately, due to the academic setbacks of his time at Ardross castle, as well as any number of other effects from his situation at the time, Austin struggled, and failed all but one of his courses in his first year. Looking back, though he feels there may have been signs even earlier, this is the period where Austin feels his schizophrenia began to develop. He felt trapped in his anxieties and depressions, and ended up simply working trivial jobs, before returning to school in the summer of 1981. From then on, Austin focused everything on his schooling, declaring Geography as his major and largely shutting himself off from everything else. Before he could graduate though, Austin fell deeper into a depression, and a period where his symptoms began to worsen; he felt as though his time had been wasted, and that there was no point to what he had done or was doing. Thankfully, things would soon turn around for Austin - if only for a time.

In 1985, Austin took a remote sensing course, during which he had an idea that would lead to one of the most amazing periods of his life: going to Antarctica in search of meteorites. Thanks to his idea of making use of remote sensing and aerial photography to cut down on the time people needed to spend physically searching the harsh Antarctic environment, Austin was invited to join the Antarctic Search for Meteorites (ANSMET). And, after pursuing and completing a Master's degree in South Dakota, and being accepted into a PhD program at the University of Texas, that's exactly what Austin did.

As could be expected, Austin's time in Antarctica was challenging, but still a highlight of his life. During his time there, Austin helped recover hundreds of meteorites - one by accidentally stopping to take a leak on it. Even though Austin's idea of utilizing remote sensing to find meteorites didn't end up working - though because of the state of technology at the time, and not because of the idea itself - Austin's time there was a success. Unfortunately, it was a taxing success for

Austin, both physically and mentally. During his time in the cold, Austin developed nerve damage in his legs, leaving him with a limp, and a permanent cough. Worse still, the stress of being in the Antarctic led to pronounced, early signs of Austin's schizophrenia. Though not the earliest signs, Austin found himself with constant headaches, dizziness, and an inability to count past 7. Of course at the time, it was hard to say what was wrong; who would expect living in the extreme conditions of the Antarctic not to cause problems, both physically and mentally? But as time would tell, there was more to it than that. Upon returning home, Austin found that due to some miscommunication or error somewhere along the way, he had been kicked out of his program at the University of Texas, because he had been away from his studies for so long. He fell into a depression, and had difficulties coping with the still fresh damage to his legs from the cold, his removal from his program, and the expectation of those around him to act as if everything was now back to 'normal.'

Austin never ended up successfully appealing the decision made by the University of Texas, despite his Father's efforts at the time to sort things out while he recovered. Instead, Austin just continued to sink into his depression, and what was the start of a struggle he would be dealing with for the rest of his life. That being said, it's hard to say what exactly 'led' to Austin's schizophrenia, whether odds are he would have developed it sooner or later because of his genetics, or if he was simply predisposed to it and the events he experienced caused it. Either way, what happened next probably didn't help.

In 1991, with his trip to the Antarctic now just a memory, Austin received an invitation to join an expedition to an archipelago in northern Russia in the Arctic Ocean, put on by the Geographical Society of the USSR. Having been previously shortlisted in 1988 for another expedition by the Soviet Government, but not ultimately getting to participate, Austin was excited for the honour. Things didn't go as planned though, as instead of being welcomed in Moscow, Austin was treated with suspicion, even having the books he brought with him as gifts questioned and accused of being western propaganda. Though there were less outwardly hostile moments in the trip, none of it went as Austin expected. Austin never made it to the expedition, instead spending his trip being escorted by one 'security' detail or another on tours through Moscow, until his apparently suspicious behaviour led to him being incarcerated. It is at this point in Austin's trip where determining what exactly happened becomes difficult, as Austin may very well have had a psychotic break while locked up in Moscow. Whether hallucination, pure truth, or some mix of the two though, Austin's trip to Moscow certainly didn't end any better than it started. While incarcerated, Austin remembers being led to a room to sit alone for a while, after which he felt ill for days. This led him to believe it may have been some put into the room to be asphyxiated, or that the room was some sort of gas chamber. Additionally, Austin believes he may have been drugged at one point, in order to get him to sign some documents - the nature of which, he is uncertain. Besides these two events though, the rest of the trip before and after are clear; eventually, the Canadian embassy sent a Hungarian woman to get Austin released. At first, Austin was suspicious of her, and believed she was simply a ploy of sorts to get him to lower his guard. However, thankfully for Austin, she was the real deal and helped negotiate his rescue. She even told Austin, upon hearing that he was suffering from a stomach ache, that it could indicate that he had been poisoned, making the entire situation that much harder to unravel.

After Austin's brief introduction to a real life spy thriller, he was returned home to Canada. However, instead of receiving support after the events he had just gone through, Austin was met with disbelief, with some of his colleagues going so far as to think he had finally lost it. As damaging as the events were, it would be the disbelief Austin faced that would send him over the edge. Austin became intent on proving to those around him what had occurred, and decided to convince them by recounting his experience in detail, to show them without a doubt that what he was saying was real. Unfortunately, forcing himself to relive the incredibly recent ordeal took an even greater toll on Austin. Going through the events of his recent ordeal over and over and over again, combined with the other stressors of his life at the time, pushed him to his limit. But he finished the book, and, as awful as the process of writing it was, things immediately after got better, with Austin even beginning to get some traction applying for a PhD program at the University of South Africa. Unfortunately, as it would turn out, things were about to get worse than they had ever been for Austin.

The improvement following the completion of his book ended up being short lived, as though Austin didn't fall apart upon completing his extensive recounting as may have been expected reading about the stress and strain it caused, it turns out that he had simply reached the calm before the storm. A short while later, as Austin was relaxing at a university bar with his friend Larry, he had a psychotic break. Upon returning from the washroom, Austin recalls noticing two women dressed all in black sitting by the bar, and recognizing that they were witches. More than that though, they seemed to be trying to signal something to Austin. Unfortunately, Austin didn't have the chance to figure out what it was they were signaling, as he was busy dealing with all the bees suddenly swarming him. Then, just as suddenly, the TV in the bar began transmitting images of the moon to Austin, directly into his mind as he recalls, and he began to feel as though he could control the direction of the program with his thoughts. After sharing these and other 'revelations' to Larry - and convincing said friend that Austin must have taken some LSD or something during his trip to the washroom - Larry decided it was time to call it a night, and walked home with Austin. Though the night was finished for Larry, Austin would continue to share what he had learned from the witches and the moon, calling his mother to tell her everything, and prompting his father to travel down to Edmonton to check on Austin.

Given the family history of schizophrenia, Ernest knew that it was either drugs or schizophrenia that led to Austin's incoherent ramblings the night before. Early the next morning, Ernest drove Austin to the hospital to find out. Initially the staff were certain Austin was simply coming off of a bad trip. Thankfully though, they kept Austin for the day, waiting for him to sober up so they could be rid of him. Except, he never did. Sadly, this didn't stop the medical staff from being rid of him anyways. Since his father was around, they passed Austin and his care off to him for "natural support" as Austin recalls, leaving Austin's poor father to make do. As can probably be guessed, this was somewhat outside of Ernest's expertise. Unsure of what to do next, but determined to help his son, Ernest took Austin to the only other place he could think of to find help or advice on what to do: church. More accurately, Ernest brought Austin to a priest at St. Joseph's, within the grounds of the University of Alberta, to figure out what to do next. Having taken care of his schizophrenic wife for so long, Ernest knew how much additional aid Austin would need, especially now. The advice given, and ultimately taken, was this: if Ernest stayed in Edmonton, then odds are any hospital he took Austin to would pawn him back off to Ernest - as such, it was the priest's advice to essentially abandon Austin, in order to leave the hospital's with no "natural support" to pass responsibility onto.

Ernest and the priest made the gamble that, if Austin went to the hospital alone - as the priest informed Ernest he could not take Austin in at the time - then the hospital would be forced to help. But it was quite the risk; with Austin in the state he was in, any number of things could have gone wrong: he could have walked into traffic, or a manhole, gotten robbed or assaulted, scared himself with a hallucination and run into any of the above or other dangers, gotten himself arrested. Odds are individuals more creative than myself could easily add to the list. But in the end Austin made it through his time alone. After wandering the streets for almost the entire day, stopping at home, getting dumped, and trying to find a manhole to crawl into along the way, Austin found himself at another church. Once there, the Usher met Austin and knew he needed help, taking him back to the hospital that, just under 24 hours ago, had kicked him out of. After the same song and dance as last time regarding the disbelief it was anything real or serious, when Austin again failed to sober up, he finally received the help he needed, and was taken to the psych ward of the hospital.

As terrible as Austin's ordeal was, with Austin feeling as though and believing that he had died at several points, things would eventually improve for him. I by no means wish to imply that this came about easily or quickly; even in care Austin was miserable, believing he had died and even been decapitated when off his medications, and feeling as though he might as well have when on them. Early in his stay at the hospital, Austin found himself relating to a dead bird that he saw outside his window, simply sitting and staring at it, and feeling a connection with the poor bird's situation. It wasn't a great time. Even though Austin was now receiving help, with the state of the medications at the time leaving feeling as though he had been practically lobotomized while taking them, the difficulty of coming to terms with this new reality and all that he had lost, and the depression that came along with it all, at the start, things were only better on paper - if then. Though he is a constant advocate for them now, decades into life with schizophrenia, Austin reached a point where he began fighting against his doctors, refusing to take his medications. Like his mother before him, Austin was ready to dig in his heels and fight, for the rest of his life if he had to, in order to avoid the medications, their side effects, their impact on him, and, most of all, against the truth of the situation. Thankfully for Austin, and everyone who he has helped since, his father was able to convince him to start taking his medications again. As awful as it all was - the drooling, the sedation, the stigma - Ernest convinced Austin to take them, warning him that if he refused to take them, he'd set himself down the same path as his mother. Austin remembers his father saying to him, " I know it's not a great option. It's close to being the worst. But it's not. Sitting like this and doing nothing is. So you can either lose or lose even more."

As awful as it all was, Ernest was right, and Austin chose to lose, at least until he could find a way to win. Which he did. Staying on his meds consistently for the past 30 years, Austin has managed to have a more impactful and fulfilling life as a schizophrenic than many able bodied and mentally 'normal' people will in twice the time. Austin has published nearly countless books and articles, both on his own, with others, and through his employment of and working with students. He has earned nearly 30 honours and awards, if not more that I'm simply unaware of, including the Order of Canada and the Order of St. Sylvester. He's met the Pope twice, has one adopted and three foster sons, and continues to go out for coffee and meet with friends, colleagues, and students whenever he can - in between his busy days of paperwork and browbeating politicians and public figures into doing what's right.

As hopeless as he was, even after speaking with his father and deciding to go back onto his medications, Austin just kept moving forward. Putting one foot in front of the other, choosing to start volunteering after figuring out the finances with the help of his doctor, and keeping at it, doing every little thing he could - especially the things that no one else wanted to step up to do. Austin found fulfillment in his work, even as he tried to relearn basic tasks and everyday living. But he pulled through, with the help of his mother and father. He got married, twice, and though the first marriage didn't end up lasting, Austin's condition ultimately had next to nothing to do with its end. And now, with Catherine, he's happier and more active than ever.

As far as Austin is concerned, everyone suffers. Everyone has to go through or live with something awful at some point or another, and he doesn't think he's anywhere close to special enough for that not to apply to him. But he took his new reality, his world ending and life changing illness, and he rolled with it. There's no reason to expect your life to be half as hectic as Austin's if you too are schizophrenic, and you can maybe even expect a somewhat easier go of it thanks to all of the improvements in medications, and the constant march towards a world with less stigma and ignorant hate. But if there is one thing to take away from Austin's life, it should be that there is hope. Stick with your medications, listen to your doctors (though feel free to shop around if you don't have faith in yours), and just keep fighting. Austin may not be the conventional, uber rich and material success that we have been taught to imagine. But he's happy. He's fulfilled. And with everything he has done and continues to do, only the willfully ignorant could deny that he is at least some kind of success.

Going forward into the rest of this book, through the various ups, downs, and facts presented along the way, keep in mind that while it will absolutely suck, potentially for quite some time, your life is still what you make of it. And Austin Mardon is living proof that you can still make quite a lot of it. As he likes to say, if he - and John Nash, who was even crazier than Austin (according to Austin) - can make it, then anyone who tries can.

Acceptance and Humour

One of the trickiest and most critical steps to take for those with Schizophrenia is developing a willingness to accept the illness. This means more than merely acknowledging that you have it, it also means accepting the limitations that may come with it. Unfortunately, there is no one size fits all checklist of all the things that you must accept about a diagnosis of Schizophrenia, because the illness treats each person differently. Some people may be comparatively "higher" or "lower" functioning, depending on factors like the severity and exact nature of the illness, the response to available medical treatments, the support system available and the personality of the person who has Schizophrenia. It's complex, but one thing will consistently undermine any attempt to move forward with the illness, and that is not whole-heartedly accepting Schizophrenia as part of who you are.

Which is not to say that you can't make a distinction between yourself and your illness. But just as it's irrational to act as though you are completely healthy when you have cancer, even if you can imagine yourself a certain way without cancer and would like to live without it, the cancer is still a part of your lived reality. So it is with any mental illness, and certainly Schizophrenia specifically. Schizophrenia is part of your world. And just like you could avoid treatment for cancer and go on living as if you don't have it, you could make a similar move with Schizophrenia, but only at great risk to yourself because you don't really have any sort of plan for limiting the negative effects of Schizophrenia. Ignoring Schizophrenia will not make it go away.

But just like with the cancer analogy, there can be more subtle ways in which you can deny that you have an illness. You can be in the hospital undergoing radiation treatments while maintaining that you are almost done with treatment and should be released any day, when in reality you have just begun. Just like our imaginary cancer patient, you can treat your illness like it's not a big deal, that a cure will be found soon, or that it's just a nagging irritation. This is not acceptance, this is closer to the bargaining stage of grief. Of course, the opposite isn't much help either—if you are overstating the effect that Schizophrenia is going to have on you and ignoring the fact that imperfect but helpful treatments are out there could leave you feeling quite depressed. And it's quite possible to bounce between these two extremes, minimizing your symptoms into false optimism before catastrophizing and taking a downward spiral into undue despair and then possibly rebounding again, and you can continue to cycle between these poles until you are willing to reach acceptance where you take a realistic outlook on the exact nature and extent of your limitations, and also the level you can reach with the best available treatment.

The news of the diagnosis can be initially quite devastating. Austin's first reaction was to withdraw from all of those around him, assuming that his life was essentially over. It would be too easy to say "cheer up, things can get better", because it's not that easy to snap out of a serious depression. However, there are people who have been in very dark places and eventually found their way out of that place. It may take more time than a person experiencing the depression would like, however, and it may involve some counselling to see that there is indeed hope that is not false. It does need to come from a more foundational place than denying that Schizophrenia is a real and substantial part of your experience; it needs to come from a conviction that life is worth living, even if there are real limits for life with Schizophrenia. But you can learn to live with those limits. Life is not only worth living if you meet every goal that you set out to accomplish, it is worth living for its own sake.

Which isn't to say you should give up on your goals immediately. You are going to have to take some time to feel out your situation before you can with any reasonable certainty know whether something you were hoping to do is unrealistic. And each goal needs to be considered individually, some will be more realistic than others. At our best, we form our goals out of who we are and what we could reasonably hope to attain, and if you could have had reason to believe you could attain your goal before a diagnosis, who says that you might not be able to get the same things done now that you know what you are dealing with? After all, it's not like a diagnosis causes you to suffer from the symptoms of Schizophrenia, they may have been there before. And yes, maybe some treatments may make certain goals more difficult, or in some unfortunate circumstances, unlikely. But the symptoms of Schizophrenia are likely to interfere with almost all goals that one might have, so there's actually a good chance that facing your diagnosis squarely, and accepting treatment, will make those goals more likely.

It is important to bring to the forefront a goal that you may not have thought much about before, but is crucial to anyone suffering from any mental illness: the goal to be as well as possible. If you have the attitude that you are willing to take the advice of doctors, try a variety of recommended treatments, and generally take maintenance of your mental health very seriously, everything else can start to fall into place. This does mean that you should take your medicine scrupulously, although if you are experiencing debilitating side effects, you can and should advocate for yourself for another treatment plan. This does mean that you should probably exercise regularly, as that seems to improve mental and physical health almost universally. And it does mean you need to take advice from doctors to heart. Being well is just going to be harder, but that doesn't mean you can't have strong mental health, it just means it takes more work to get there.

So what if something in taking care of your mental health will significantly interfere with or even prevent accomplishing one of your most cherished life goals? Well, three things. One, maybe it just means that you will have to focus on other goals for now. Two, it's possible to come up with new goals at any point in your life, and while you shouldn't try to force this to happen, you can look forward to having new things to look forward to. Three, just because something is not possible now doesn't mean that advancements in treatment may not make it possible in the future. Perhaps it won't happen, but then again, it is also possible that it will. Think more in terms of setting something aside for now rather than burying a dream for good.

Of course, one of the most important tools to overcoming difficult situations is having a sense of humour. If you are just constantly brooding over your situation and the many things you will never do as a result of how your life is irreparably changed, you are likely to slip into depression. It's hard to constantly ponder negativity and not get depressed. Having a sense of humour can be a sharp weapon against taking your situation, and yourself, too seriously.

There is an opposite extreme to be avoided. If you never take your situation seriously, it's hard to imagine how you will find the motivation to stick to your medication, for instance. And if you are always the butt of your own jokes, it can develop into a lack of self-respect which can then lead to unhealthy behaviour. The goal with humour is to avoid taking yourself and your situation with grim seriousness constantly because that becomes oppressive. And when you point your sense of humour at Schizophrenia itself, it creates a relationship to your illness that makes it seem less daunting and all-encompassing.

There is something about making a joke about something which dislodges it from a place of being an all-consuming, all-important thing. You can often tell what is sacred to a person by what they refuse to joke about. If you can make a joke about your condition, it signals to yourself that Schizophrenia is not some kind of temperamental and capricious god that controls your life. It is just something you live with, so why not have a little fun at the illness' expense? And while you can probably take too many liberties with this, maybe humour can be a way to not take you and your struggle with Schizophrenia too seriously. Some people use self-deprecating humour to the point where it becomes uncomfortable, but it can be a good way to combat the self-absorption which can creep into a person's life if they have been mulling the nature of existence and suffering for too long.

It's also worth noting the obvious, that joking about something can just make you feel better. While making jokes about something can signal that it's something not to be taken seriously, for most people, not taking mental illness seriously is not the issue. The issue tends to be viewing mental illness as some kind of death sentence, and making light of your illness and a little self-deprecation about how you interact with that illness can brighten the mood. It also helps remind you that you can take pleasure in life, and enjoy it, and again, this can break the monotony of endless brooding.

Of course, crossing the line between making light of yourself and Schizophrenia into mocking and belittling may not be a problem for you specifically, but it may be something that others do, especially if you signal that it's okay to joke about such things. Humour does make a serious point, and if the point is that you are a mental invalid because of your illness, you can rightfully confront someone for making inappropriate jokes. However, you should be very specific about what it was about the joke that crossed the line, and not that it was a joke about you or your mental illness. If it comes across that it's okay for you to make those sorts of jokes but not for other people to make the same kinds of jokes, people will be rightfully irritated.

These two considerations are in the same chapter because the need to accept and take your situation and illness seriously and your need to have a little fun and not always take everything so completely seriously tend to pull in opposite directions, and it's important to affirm both. You can be a well-treated and depressed Schizophrenic because you just always take everything so completely seriously, or you can treat everything like it's one big joke and have a good time, but leave your Schizophrenia virtually untreated. The key is to find a middle ground of tension between the two extremes. You have to take things seriously enough to get the right treatment, but lightly enough that the particulars don't become depressing. It's a balancing act, but it is a balancing act that can be done.

Romantic Relationships

What may be one of the most pressing questions after a diagnosis of Schizophrenia is how this will impact intimate relationships? It's also a question that unfolds quite differently depending on the state of one's romantic life at the moment. If one is already in some kind of relationship, does this mean that the relationship is in jeopardy? And if one is not in such a relationship, but does want to be in such a relationship, what are the chances of that happening?

The good news is that if you are already romantically involved, unless that relationship is very new, that person should already know of the symptoms that led to a diagnosis of Schizophrenia. You can honestly say to the other person, "I'm the same person I was before the diagnosis, it's just that now there's an explanation for the reason I am the way that I am". This is true, and if a person was happy to be with you before, you should be in a better position to move forward after a diagnosis, because you can be given more proven coping mechanisms for Schizophrenia. The only thing that has changed is that you now have a name for some of your struggles. If the person is unwilling to look past the stereotypes of Schizophrenia and see you as a person first and a Schizophrenic second, is this really a person who you want to be with for the long haul?

Of course getting a Schizophrenia diagnosis right when a relationship is new is awkward timing. I assumed in the previous paragraph that the person in your existing relationship is close enough to you to know about your diagnosis roughly around the time that you receive it. This may not be true if a relationship you are in is new or hasn't taken a serious turn yet. The question of whether to disclose is tricky. You probably will have to if you want the relationship to take a more serious turn. But there's no specific timeline on when any given relationship might go that direction. It is possible to end this kind of relationship because you don't feel the other person is willing to commit to someone with Schizophrenia, but you still likely owe them some explanation for why you are ending the relationship. If you are uncomfortable with explaining that it is Schizophrenia, you could honestly say that it is for sensitive medical reasons you are uncomfortable discussing. This is true without forcing you to expose something about yourself you are not ready to.

The situation may be much different if you are not in a relationship, and want to be, when you receive your diagnosis. On one hand, it may be a bit much to lead off every conversation with every potential romantic partner with "hi I'm so-and-so and I'm a Schizophrenic", but it's not honest to hide your diagnosis from someone you hope to have a trusting relationship with either. It will undermine your relationship to be hiding the elephant in the room, and all good relationships, not just romantic ones, need to be based on trust. You need to find a time between the initial meeting and taking steps towards a more serious relationship to tell the person. But don't wait for a perfect moment, because the perfect moment may never come. Having a discussion about your diagnosis that begins awkwardly is still better than not having the discussion at all. Just make sure you are in a place where you can potentially have a lengthy conversation if necessary—you don't know how much you may have to educate the other person about Schizophrenia in general and your experience in particular. You also don't know what sort of misconceptions you will have to gently disabuse the other person of. Pick a time and place where you are less likely to be interrupted or need to rush off somewhere else if possible, but again, don't let the perfect become the enemy of the good.

That said, you shouldn't disclose your diagnosis if you are uncomfortable with doing so. But it's important to understand what kind of discomfort you are feeling, and why. Do you feel uncomfortable telling strangers because you know there are a lot of negative or just plain inaccurate stereotypes out there, and don't want to be immediately associated with them? That's perfectly fair. If that's the case, you may feel more comfortable sharing once you get to know a person and find them to be open-minded to what you have to say, and willing to take your word rather than cling to hurtful prejudices. On the other hand, do you feel uncomfortable telling any person under any circumstances ever that you have Schizophrenia, even the most supportive of family and mental health care workers? That may be a sign of needing to work on self-acceptance. If that's the case, you might need to grow more comfortable in your own skin before you seriously consider a romantic relationship. If you are not ready to admit who you are to those who have earned the right to be trusted, how can you have the confidence to simply be yourself around them? You are probably the last person who needs to be reminded that constantly wearing a (social) mask is exhausting, so why would you bring that work into your day-to-day existence?

Austin has had some experience with disclosing his Schizophrenia. He initially met Catherine on a Catholic dating website, and after they had hit it off, and the relationship was starting to look more serious in nature (and it's worth remembering the Catholic website was specifically for those looking to eventually get married, so there was a safe assumption that both of them were looking for a permanent relationship), Austin tried to get Catherine to stumble across his Schizophrenia by suggesting she google him, knowing that some of the articles about him also discussed his Schizophrenia diagnosis. Catherine eventually did so, but didn't read any of the articles that specifically discussed Schizophrenia. So Austin knew he had to tell her directly, which was understandably intimidating, given how much awkward to despicable treatment he had received for being labeled as a Schizophrenic. Austin tells the story in his own words, taken from Thriving from Schizophrenia:

"In the beginning, I was afraid to tell her that I had schizophrenia. I knew from past experience that the word often sends people running. When I finally got up the courage, her only comment was, "That's interesting. So what?" I assumed she simply didn't understand what the word meant. I didn't know at the time that she had vast experience dealing with those with serious mental illnesses in her legal practice. I kept trying to explain what having schizophrenia would mean for our relationship, and finally she said in exasperation, 'if you are trying to scare me off, you'll have to find something else. I don't scare easily.' I remember sitting with my father that afternoon crying in joy that God had brought a woman into my life with the capacity for unconditional love." --Chapter 8, Thriving with Schizophrenia.

Many of the day-to-day issues of a successful long-term relationship may have little to nothing to do with Schizophrenia itself. Mental illness or not, there are some serious adjustments that need to be made in living with anyone, quirks of personality that may not bother you but are burdensome for your partner. For instance, Austin was initially afraid to let Catherine into his house because it was a disorganized mess, which if it is related to his Schizophrenia, it is rather indirectly. Anyone might be messy and have a disorganized house, Schizophrenia or mental illness is hardly a prerequisite. And there can be dozens of other things, large and small, that might be an issue for a couple trying to keep their commitment to each other and inhabit the same place at the same time.

Communication and compromise are crucial. There may be some aspects factors in the relationship, such as a mental illness, which can't be abolished but only managed. Then there are other things that are skills that can be worked on, like maintaining a degree of cleanliness in the house. Properly identifying which things cannot fundamentally go away and which can be overcome, and not categorizing something wrongly, is important. But even if you know what needs to be managed and what could be overcome, you still need a realistic plan, and a plan that is communicated adequately to both partners. It's much easier to say than it is to do; it is very easy to end up with two completely different conceptions of what is going to be done between spouses simply because a handful of words were interpreted differently than they were meant. It can be quite an unpleasant surprise when you realize that you were both operating under completely different assumptions. And sometimes, it's not even words being interpreted differently, but rather a lack of any sort of communication leading to different expectations. This is as common as it is frustrating.

It's not that a relationship cannot work if one or both of you is Schizophrenic, because all relationships take work and require negotiation as to how to properly be together. However, relationships require a commitment, and that includes not only a commitment to the other person, but also a commitment to seeking the best possible treatment. There can be mitigating factors in how effective any given possible treatments are to a person with Schizophrenia. That isn't the part you can control, so if your medications and other forms of treatment are not as effective as you would hope, there's no need to feel any guilt over that. But what you can control is your openness to treatment and being willing to trust the right medical professionals (is it possible you may just have a bad doctor, which may require a change, but don't just jump to that conclusion either). You must be ready to commit to the demands of the best available treatment and follow through with whatever is recommended to manage your symptoms. This is not just an act of personal care, it also represents your personal willingness to commit to being in the best possible shape to care for your significant other. If you don't take your regiment seriously (which doesn't mean you can't slip up, you're still human), it communicates to your significant other that you are uncaring about the potentially destructive elements of Schizophrenia.

At the same time, until a day comes where there is a cure, doing your best should be enough for the other person in a relationship. Schizophrenia can be treated but it does not simply go away, and the other person should accept the fact that you are indeed doing everything you can in order to keep Schizophrenia from running your life. If the other person sees you as primarily a Schizophrenic case, and not as a person who just happens to suffer from Schizophrenia, the relationship is in trouble. Schizophrenics are as diverse a population as any, and the way that any given Schizophrenic's illness interacts with their personality is going to vary widely. You still are going to have dreams, desires, thoughts, and feelings that are wholly your own, and the fact that you also happen to have a mental illness doesn't change the fact that, like in any relationship, this needs to be respected and even nurtured. If you can find someone who likes who you are, understands and sympathizes with how Schizophrenia affects your life, and is willing to support you in what you hope to do in the world, you have probably found a keeper.

However, no matter how much you follow your treatment regimen, how much you focus on clear communication, or how much you endeavour to take care of the other person's needs, there are inevitably going to be some difficulties. There is conflict in every romantic relationship, and this is especially true of the ones that are committed. No amount of love prevents conflict, and paradoxically, the more love there is in a relationship, the more potential there is for conflict. And while it sometimes comes about because you are not being considerate or loving the other person the way you should, it is at times unavoidable. The important thing is that when you fight, you must fight fair. Don't resort to name-calling, accusations or pointed sarcasm. You need to keep calm, even when the other person is pushing all your buttons. It's a skill, but a crucially important one, to handle conflict in reasonable and thoughtful ways. And since it is a skill, it is something that you can get better at. You can learn something from every yelling match. Over time, you can decrease the temperature and manage your conflict. Just don't set expectations that you will stamp out conflict altogether, this should be perfectly possible to live with.

The real enemy of any kind of relationship, romantic or not, is insisting that things be perfect. There are no perfect spouses or houses, families or lives. All that expecting perfection will do is disappoint you with how much better everything should be, and it will undermine a relationship like few other things. You need to be willing to see goodness—inside yourself, inside your spouse and in the world—regardless of whether or not something could objectively be better. As soon as you let go of the expectation that things should be ideal, you will find that things are much better than they could be, not just worse than they theoretically might be. Allow things to be what they are, not what you would cast them as in a frozen and spotless world that exists only inside your mind, and this will allow them to grow. And nothing is more stultifying to flourishing than constantly being judged for imperfection. Imperfect things are the only things capable of growth. You can only flourish if the haze of seeing through a lens of an imaginary perfect world is cleared away. Avoid perfectionism fastidiously.

The longing for unconditional love is universal. It is ultimately this longing that leads us to seek a partner, but it's worth remembering that even if you go for long periods without having a romantic relationship in your life, it is ultimately the life-giving nature of unconditional love that can sustain a person through even the most intense suffering. While an intense source of this can be a committed romantic relationship, it is not the only place to look for this, as we will discuss in the following chapter.

Platonic Relationships

While there are only so many people that you can be romantically involved with over a lifetime, there really is no limit to the number of friendships that one can have. However, a problem with developing a wide variety of friendships is that it is possible that people can be your "friend" for the wrong reasons. And one very clear way to sort true friends from those who are just hanging on for other reasons is to have a mental illness with all the stigma that is attached to it. Losing friends may seem like a downside, but knowing those who actually care about you from those who do not can actually be quite the blessing.

Losing friendships hurts. There's no getting around that, and it can be very hard to have people that you thought were there for you, through thick and thin, suddenly disappear from your life. While this can happen with a Schizophrenia diagnosis, again, the upside is you have a better idea of who the people are that truly care about who you are, and aren't in it for something like status or the way you happen to make them feel about themselves. There is no getting around it that the process of losing friends, especially if it happens all at once is difficult. But you needn't have any hard feelings towards them, because while they might not have been as close to you as you thought, you can still wish them well and hope that they lead good lives. It's not a good thing to abandon a friend at a difficult time, but one bad action doesn't add up to being a bad person.

Of course, it's important to remember that the basis for any kind of friendship is honesty. While you can have casual relationships where you don't disclose your illness, it's difficult to be close to someone without being honest about a major element of your experience of life, even if you fear that the other person might abandon you upon finding out. This isn't to say that you should just go ahead and confess your diagnosis to everyone in the hopes of laying a foundation for a strong relationship—if you feel uncomfortable disclosing your illness, that may be a sign that you are not ready to deepen that relationship. You will likely need to admit that you have an illness to those closest to you, and those that you are growing close to. Exactly how you decide to go about this is up to you; you can be as direct or indirect as you like, but if you do try to do it indirectly, just be sure that your method actually communicates what you hope it to communicate.

However, you have to get used to disclosing your illness, because chances are that you will have to do it more than once. If you are uncomfortable with the prospect of admitting that you have a mental illness to anyone, regardless of circumstance and how you expect them to react, then you probably need to work on your acceptance of yourself first. Nobody wants to be misunderstood, but you also have to be willing to trust that at least SOME people are willing to take an understanding disposition and won't judge you for having Schizophrenia. You might be disappointed, finding someone to be prejudiced when you hoped they would be understanding, but the only way to avoid encountering these disappointing moments is to withdraw from society altogether, and I guarantee that will just leave you and everyone who loves you unhappy. You can be discerning about who you tell and when you tell them but being selective is much healthier than simply avoiding all opportunities to get hurt altogether.

There can be benefits to opening up. There are often things that the people, who you tell about your illness, may only feel comfortable confessing after you have opened up and shown some vulnerability yourself. It may allow you to have some franker and deeper relationships. Also, some people may become your biggest champion, knowing that you are a worthwhile person who just happens to have an illness, and should be seen and treated as such. You need these sorts of people because they will often be the ones who will cheer you on right as you feel on the verge of giving up. Great gains will often require you to take some risk, which is true for everyone, not just those with Schizophrenia.

If it's too much for you to keep up with everyone in your life, it's okay to take a step back. This does not mean withdrawing entirely, but it may mean going to fewer social engagements for a while, maybe missing a family gathering when you have little to no energy, or just doing fewer things. You do need to engage with the people in your life, but you need not engage in such a way that it runs you ragged. Your social relationships should energize you, even if you're an introvert (which probably means your socializing should be smaller in scope and focus on those you are closest to rather than people you only sort of know), and if you find that your social life is draining you more than a little, you have probably overcommitted to social engagements. Just be cautious that this doesn't cross the line into social withdrawal. The difference is that if you've just been too socially active for your temperament and level of gregariousness, after a few days or couple weeks of not being too social, you should feel recharged and ready to re-engage. If you're finding you're still wishing to avoid social engagement after a decent length of a break, you might want to consult with a mental health professional to see if you are suffering from some additional mental health complications like depression. You may have to consider pushing yourself to take a few steps to get yourself back out there again. If you are suffering from depression (and you can go through a depressive episode without necessarily having depression as a mental illness), depending on how deep it runs, pushing yourself may not seem possible, but this is why you should at least talk to someone who can discern the symptoms of depression or other mood disorders. Nothing about having Schizophrenia prevents you from developing other mental illnesses, unfortunately. And just like with Schizophrenia, it's better to know than to not know and suffer from the symptoms without having a plan of action for treating them. Don't be content with pat answers for why your mood or functioning may seem off or different from how it should be, as any given mental illness can be comorbid with other mental illnesses, cognitive and/or learning disorders or ADHD. You're going to function the way you normally do regardless, so it's just best to figure out the full scope of what you are dealing with.

To be not just a friend, but a good friend, usually means giving into a relationship. A lot of ways in which this is done may already be things you are doing, such as actively listening, taking opportunities to celebrate, doing something that *they* find fun, having time to talk to them, and generally enjoying their company. There may be hindrances to this, such as difficulty with reading body language, but if you are trying your best, most people will notice and forgive an occasional foible, especially as they get to know you and understand that certain limitations are just a part of what you struggle with. But you do need to give back, in whatever ways you can, if you want to get the most out of your relationship. Just beware that some people will let you give and give in a relationship and never give back themselves. Such parasitic activity is not helped by you continuing to prop up the relationship with your efforts, and if they continue to show disinterest in reciprocating your care, it's probably a relationship that you should let go.

But what if a Schizophrenia diagnosis puts a previously close relationship, sometimes even with family, in jeopardy? Well, unfortunately you can't by sheer force of will make any relationship work. There are going to be some people that will refuse to treat you properly due to your diagnosis, and you will likely only make it worse by trying to force them to see reason. If they were genuinely open to being persuaded, they wouldn't be putting the relationship under major strain. If you pray at all, pray for them. And then you will likely have to hold them at a distance because of the damage they can do. If someone genuinely has a change of heart, they will have to come to terms with the way they have treated you in the past and will want to apologize. But that's on them and their conscience, and you can't act as a substitute conscience. Your job is to judge whether or not there is enough trust to have any kind of close relationship at all.

There is no reason you can't simply enjoy strong relationships for what they are and for how they enrich life. Many of the best and most memorable moments are formed with friends, many hobbies are social either directly or indirectly and most people get more out of their hobbies if they share the experience. It's also just plain better for your mental health to surround yourself with people that you can trust.

If you're tempted to think of yourself as someone who doesn't have much to offer because you have Schizophrenia, you may want to reconsider. Even if you did have nothing to offer as a friend, you would be a worthless friend all on your own, Schizophrenia or no Schizophrenia! (This is a joke.) It really can be hard to see your own positive qualities, since for many of us, focusing on our negative aspects is sort of the default setting for how we process ourselves in the world. But we instinctively make friends because we recognize good qualities in others, and often familiar qualities, and you shouldn't be so shocked when others recognize your good qualities. It takes a lot of work to have no redeeming qualities, and frankly, you're probably not disciplined enough to have developed into such a consistent dud. (Again, this is a joke. Mostly. Having no redeeming qualities is actually hard to pull off.)

It's also just nice to have parts of your life that are not… just about the nuts and bolts of making the best go of it with Schizophrenia. Yes, there are health benefits to keeping an active social life (which does not mean you have to be the life of the party, sometimes "active social life" can mean reading books in silence around other people you're comfortable with), but part of what makes a social life a social life is the fact that it is done for the sake of enjoying the relationships. Making everything in your life sorted into the buckets of "good for dealing with Schizophrenia" or "bad for dealing with Schizophrenia" can make your life very one-note and wear you down fast. Some things are just good in and of themselves, and being around other people who are generally less repugnant than average is one of those things. Hobbies and art would be other such categories, but we deal with that elsewhere in this book.

Not everybody gets lucky in love, but just about everyone can find good friends and develop good friendships. And for those in your family who are willing to support you, their help can be invaluable. It is said that it takes a village to raise a child, but the saying can probably be expanded to it taking a village to live a full life, Schizophrenia or no. You may have to be a bit more discerning about who you trust as a person with a mental illness, but as long as you don't let that caution turn into outright avoidance, you should be able to have rich relationships with those around you. Don't let a diagnosis become an excuse for missing out of one of the most enriching elements of life.

Hobbies

Hobbies are an essential part of self-care when dealing with schizophrenia. They can serve as excellent mental distractions to treat negative symptoms, and active hobbies will keep you physically healthy. Research on hobbies assisting with schizophrenia symptoms is limited, although a study published in 2018 on holistic management of schizophrenia symptoms states that a combination of medication and recreation treatment is crucial for those with schizophrenia.

Having a hobby is more than just a coping mechanism. Often, people with schizophrenia are unable to have a full-time job. Having a good hobby can help to alleviate boredom when alone. This can help with onset of symptoms - if you find symptoms becoming stronger when your mind is idle, then keeping yourself busy can certainly be helpful. The only problem is that it can be difficult to find a hobby you like if you don't already have one.

I talked to Austin Mardon about hobbies, and asked about the importance of them. He agreed that having hobbies is important, but what's more important is having something that gets you out and socializing. Having a good social framework is critical for anybody with mental illness, not just schizophrenia, as we all need someone to turn to when times are tough. Austin recommended volunteering, joining a center near you, or joining a church group. Churches should always be welcoming to everyone, and can be a great place to start building a social support system.

Another way to get started with hobbies is by volunteering. People always need volunteers - whether you volunteer at a local shelter or a sporting event, volunteering is hugely beneficial. It provides a sense of community, and the satisfaction of contributing to your community. That satisfaction can be enough for many to fall in love with volunteer work, and you may just find something new that you enjoy!

Here in Edmonton, there is a section on the city website for volunteer opportunities. This would be a good place to start - check your city's website for local volunteering opportunities. Often, doctors, psychiatrists and medical professionals will also have information on where to get started with volunteering. Austin's advice is the same - do some research online for what's available near you, or go to a local church or outreach center.

When I asked Austin about what hobbies he does or does not recommend, he also mentioned that it's important to push your boundaries. New experiences exercise the mind, helping to distract you from your current symptoms and reducing the severity of future symptoms. Austin recommended something like Habitat for Humanity - it gets you outside, helps you meet new people, provides a new experience (unless you've helped build a house before), and gets you some physical exercise.

On that note, physical exercise is also hugely important. In a 2019 study, researchers found that physical exercise improved cognition, negative symptoms, and functional outcomes (i.e. makes everyday living easier), as well as reducing side effects from medication, such as obesity and diabetes. Physical activity can be hard to start, and hard to keep up. The best advice is to start small. Start by doing light exercises in your home, or going for a walk if it's nice outside. By gradually increasing the intensity of your exercise, you'll find it much easier to stick with it.

Physical exercise can also become a hobby! Many people find joy in heading to the gym every day, walking, running, rock climbing, swimming, and many more activities. Physical activity not only helps with your physical health, but your mental health as well, making it a crucial part of self-care for anyone, and especially those afflicted by mental illness.

In my conversation with Austin, I asked him to give some advice on how to deal with boredom, as this can be a huge problem for those with schizophrenia. Austin's advice is to develop and engage in a social framework - that is, find yourself a group, small or large, of people you can trust. A good social framework can help in all aspects of life. We talked about how to begin forming a good social group, by volunteering, or joining an outreach center or church group. Austin's final piece of advice is to not lean on just one person - it's not healthy for either of you. If you can, try your best to develop a group - that way, everyone can lean on each other, and create a sort of 'social safety net.' This ensures that no matter what you're going through, there is always someone there to go through it with you.

So, to summarize, there are a few key aspects of hobbies that you're looking for. First, you want a hobby that helps you socialize and create a social framework. To accomplish this, it's recommended to try volunteering, or joining a church group or outreach center. Second, it's important to push your boundaries and experience new things. We suggested something such as Habitat for Humanity, but a new experience is truly anything that is new to you. That could be working at a food bank, or volunteering at a library. If you've never done it before, it's worth it to try! Lastly, we looked at the importance of physical exercise. Physical activity helps your physical and mental health, and can become a new hobby that you enjoy, if you just take the time to find what kind of activity works for you. This goes along with the previous point, trying new things is always beneficial!

Finally, it's important to manage your expectations. In the same way that it's unrealistic for a double amputee to go rock climbing (although, not impossible), there may be some activities that are unrealistic to expect you to do, and that's okay! Everyone, not just those with mental illness, needs to take a look at what is possible for them and adjust their outlook to fit within the realm of possibility. Success looks different for everyone, and as long as you feel successful, you are!

Art and Music

The idea of using art and music as therapy for mental illness is a relatively new one, at least in terms of scientific research. However, now that research on this matter is happening more often, we are learning that it can be very beneficial. The Music Therapy Association of British Columbia (MTABC) lists schizophrenia as one of the main illnesses that can benefit from music therapy, as music therapy has been shown to help 'ground' those who may be experiencing mania or psychosis. But this isn't the only benefit of art and music as therapy - self-expression helps in many aspects of life.

When I asked Austin about the idea of using art and music as therapy, he said that it was important to have an artistic outlet, as "it touches parts of the soul that aren't rational." Austin also said it can be effective because it can stimulate emotions, as well as memories, which both help to calm us down and bring us in touch with ourselves. Austin's wife, Catherine, suffers from PTSD and uses music as a form of self-therapy, which Austin says helps her to cope with day-to-day symptoms of PTSD. This just goes to show that art and music are helpful for many different mental illnesses - although remember that everyone is different, and what works for others may not work for you!

Before we discuss how to go about trying art and music therapy, we should talk briefly about how and why it benefits those with schizophrenia or other mental illnesses. Art therapy is an overarching term, and could include any kind of self-expression, like drawing, dancing, singing, playing an instrument, or creative writing. In a 2005 study, researchers talked to 24 art therapists to discuss how it impacts their patients. While the researcher pointed out that the therapists often didn't formally assess outcomes, they did unanimously agree that "art therapy was effective in achieving improvements in subjective well-being of people diagnosed with schizophrenia". The important word here is 'subjective,' meaning the patient found that they felt a positive impact in how they see themselves and their illness. This alone I think is reason enough for everyone to try art therapy in some capacity.

I also asked Austin if he finds that art and music are helpful for those with schizophrenia. He told me that it can be hugely beneficial. In fact, Austin said that some people with schizophrenia wear headphones constantly, in order to distract themselves from negative symptoms, such as hearing voices. This can be an effective tactic if going out in public or lack of stimulation is a trigger for your symptoms. Additionally, Austin thinks that it is important for everyone to have some sort of artistic outlet, as self-expression can be powerful and bring you in touch with yourself. This concept of 'grounding,' 'improving subjective well-being,' and 'bringing you in touch with yourself' was consistent among the two studies I looked at, and Austin himself. It seems, then, that using art and music as therapy should be beneficial to anyone who tries.

Now that we've gone over the benefits of art and music, let's talk about how to get started. It's important to remember that the result is not nearly as important as the process, especially if you've just started. What matters is the act of self-expression, and as an added bonus seeing yourself get better will provide a feeling of satisfaction. Keeping that in mind, don;t be afraid to try whatever appeals to you.

Playing a musical instrument can unfortunately be an expensive hobby to just pick up, unless you choose to use the free instrument that everyone has - your voice! Otherwise, if you have an instrument, can afford one, or have a family member or someone in your social circle who has one that they would lend to you, then it's time to find a way to learn. Of course, traditional music lessons at a music store or school is an excellent option. You could go to your nearest music store, or look online for a local musician willing to teach. If cost is a concern, there are a lot of ways to learn online these days. For example, justinguitar.com provides free guitar lessons, and they are of great quality. YouTube is also a good option - it's always free, and chances are you can find someone teaching any instrument.

If you want a more guided experience, you can look to music therapy. Music therapy is a regulated career in Canada and many other parts of the world. Music therapists help guide you through the musical process, ensuring you get therapeutic benefit out of it. Having someone helping you personally also allows the music therapist to tailor the therapy session to your needs specifically, and, as mentioned above, the benefits of this process can be substantial.

As mentioned earlier in this chapter, Austin told me that some people with schizophrenia wear headphones and listen to music all day as a way of coping with symptoms. I thought it would be important to expand on this just a little bit. While creating music and art is a valuable hobby that can help in many areas of life, you can't always have your art with you. So, forming an emotional attachment to music can be incredibly beneficial. As Austin said, it can help distract you from symptoms, such as voices, and make you more comfortable in public spaces. In addition to this, listening to music that sparks a strong emotional reaction in you can be a great tool to help you vent after a frustrating day, or calm down after an exciting one. Listening to music that connects with you can serve as a stand-in when other forms of self-therapy are unreachable - but, like with anything, it's important not to become too reliant on just one thing!

The other half of art and music is much more broad. The term 'art' is very general, and includes all types of self-expression, including music. But, since art therapy and music therapy are two distinct forms of therapy, in this context 'art' will exclude the art of music. That being said, art can mean dancing, drawing, painting, model-making, creative writing, journaling, crafts, woodworking, and so much more. Anything that you decide is right for you is valid, since the act of self-expression is the important aspect.

Luckily, art is usually significantly easier to get into than music. For instance, creative writing or drawing is as easy as having a pencil and paper. This process of just sitting down and practicing art is valuable. It can be used as a distraction during negative symptoms, become something you look forward to, and provide a long-lasting feeling of satisfaction. However, motivation can be a problem for some people, especially if you're learning something new. Thankfully, there exists a plethora of classes for art, from painting to sculpting to woodworking. Here in Edmonton, we have the City Arts Centre, which actually provides free art classes for families and individuals of all ages. If you're not in Edmonton, take a look online for free classes near you, there's a good chance your city or an organization in your city has something for you! Group classes are an even better choice, since they can help expand your social framework.

Much like music therapy, professional art therapy is also available. It offers much of the same benefits of music therapy, with a personal therapy plan and a certified professional, with the added benefit of being more accessible. Art therapists can utilize many forms of art to help you along your journey, and show you how your art is positively influencing you.

To recap - the benefits of using art and music as therapy are substantial. Of course, research on this is in its infancy but current findings all agree that there is some benefit to be found for almost anyone who utilizes this type of therapy. Benefits include improved self-image, improved coping mechanisms, long-term satisfaction, and much more. We covered how to get started in art and music, by seeking out free or affordable classes, or by learning with friends. And finally, we discussed professional and structured therapy options, which can be even more beneficial than self-therapy. Using art and music as therapy or as a hobby could be the missing piece you need - all you have to do is try!

Religion and Spirituality

Although the subject may appear to be more important to some than to others, there are some challenges surrounding religion and spirituality that Schizophrenia raises. After all, Schizophrenia can often take explicitly religious forms, and that could serve as a temptation to either sink further into the voices and images that come from the illness, or inspire the opposite tactic with fleeing from everything that is spiritual and religious because it is associated with Schizophrenic symptoms.

The fact of the matter is that spirituality is part of the human experience, and while there may be concerns about accepting religiously themed voices or images as really being there, why is this any more or less dangerous than voices or images of a non-explicitly religious nature? Does it make sense to likewise eject all people from one's life because some of them might be hallucinations? Or to stop communicating through a phone or email because one might hallucinate a communication? The proper response in these cases seems to not be outright rejection, but rather caution, and that seems to be the prudent course when it comes to the realm of the religious.

If anything, a major life event like a Schizophrenia diagnosis is a great time to do some spiritual searching. What is it that makes life meaningful? What role might you have to play in the world, if any? What is a good life? These are questions that are turned over in the minds of many, professional and lay people alike. Going to philosophy is not a bad idea, but when you go to religions, they offer a rich history of invigorating the lives of wide swaths of people, especially those that come from long historical traditions (even those that may be more recent branches or forms of an older religion). The nice thing about standing in a religious tradition is that you know that in dealing with life's most pressing and difficult questions, you stand as another in a long line of people who have wrestled with the same problems with, in and through a religious tradition. That's incredibly valuable.

Of course, one has to be careful with the aspects of a religion or spirituality that most explicitly deal with things that overlap with Schizophrenic symptoms. There are aspects of some religions that involve visions, or hearing the voice of God or some other supernatural being, and there are obvious reasons to be skeptical if someone with Schizophrenia has a similar experience. This need not lead to skepticism of these sorts of experiences in general, but it's far more probable that if you suffer from Schizophrenia and hear a voice or see a vision of some sort of otherworldly creature, it's more likely coming from the illness rather than any sort of authentic religious experience. This is not the denial of the supernatural per se so much as it is an affirmation of probability, and the more probable explanation for a person who suffers from Schizophrenia is that it comes from Schizophrenia. Leave the prophet business to those who have a better signal to noise ratio.

But what if it's both? If you believe in God, could not God operate in such a way that he causes you to hear His authentic voice, and not something merely from the illness? He theoretically could, and you could consider it possible, but it's not like there is a foolproof way of telling whether the message has any origin other than merely your illness. If the message seems to affirm the teachings of your religious persuasion, rather than thrusting odd beliefs on you, and if it's not filling you with fear and paranoia, it might be possible to view it with less suspicion. But there can be a real danger if you start seeking these experiences out, especially if that leads you to want to discontinue your use of your medication. A certain degree of distanced ambivalence may be the best approach, no matter what the exact nature of the religious experiences you have.

One of the most important aspects of any kind of spirituality is a sense of gratitude. It can be quite easy to get caught up in the struggles of mental illness and forget to be thankful for all the good that is in one's life. Gratitude often has little correlation with how easy one's life is— gratitude comes more from the intention to understand life and all that comes with it as a gift, even if there is suffering along the way. This is crucial to any kind of spirituality, and certainly a key building block in strong mental health. If you want others to not see you as Schizophrenia that happens to have a person, but a person who happens to have Schizophrenia, it's important you be consistent and see your own life as being about more than just what challenges mental illness brings.

There may be a natural inclination to push back on the advice to think of all things with a sense of gratitude. After all, it can be easy to think of dealing with a mental illness as being sort of unfairly picked upon by the fates to suffer needlessly. "How come everyone else gets to have a great life and I'm stuck as a Schizophrenic?" However, the root of such thinking can come from jealousy and entitlement. Jealousy directed at others who seem to have it better than you, and entitlement for assuming that just because you are alive, you are entitled to having it easy in the way most other people seem to have it easy. But what is it, exactly, that proves that you deserve anything at all? You can't even create the conditions for your own existence, let alone prove that you have some metaphysical right to the good life, or even just the normal life. Life itself is provided for you in a way that you cannot force it to be there for you. Life, in any measure, is miraculous, and it is substantially better when it is viewed that way.

There can be certain unfortunate moments in life with Schizophrenia if you have a prominent place in your life for spirituality. Austin, who had been a devout Catholic before he started experiencing some of the more apparent symptoms of Schizophrenia, had this encounter in which his illness caused him to fundamentally misunderstand an encounter with another person while experiencing psychosis:

"Austin's delirium was uninterrupted during this time, and he recalls approaching a man who was mowing his lawn. Austin asked him: 'Is God here?' The man replied, 'God is everywhere,' and Austin remembers the amazement that he felt after hearing those words. As Austin tells me this, he chuckles at the memory and says, 'you know, I felt like this guy really understood, he really got what I was about.'" – Life Before Diagnosis, *Tea With the Mad Hatter*

But this brings up something important. Austin doesn't look back at the memory of thinking of this moment as a profound religious moment with self-contempt or shame or regret. If you truly believe that this is an illness, you should also believe that you shouldn't be ashamed of any sort of disconnect from reality. Although people tend to take religion very seriously, and rightfully so, you can still take it with a certain lightness without straying into blasphemy or irreverence. The key is who or what is the butt of the joke—if you're just mocking spiritual things because they are spiritual, that's probably inappropriate. If you are taking a humorous approach to yourself, and some of the comical ways that people interact with the sacred, it's probably a good place to be at. You can only take yourself so completely seriously for so long before being yourself starts to become a burden, and this can be especially a danger in the realm of spirituality and religion. It takes some tact and wisdom, but part of the wisdom of religion is that there are things besides yourself to concern yourself with, so maybe take yourself with a grain of salt, so to speak. The holy things are holy, but then there's us, so it's probably appropriate to take ourselves not as gravely important as we might tend to.

Spirituality is a part of life, and just because it is possible to have some inauthentic religious experiences doesn't mean you can't also have some authentic ones. For someone without Schizophrenia, hearing the voice of God doesn't necessarily have to seem literal or like a threat, but the yearnings of the soul should be taken seriously no matter the conditions. A distinction has to be made between things that trace back to experiencing Schizophrenia and the longings that all human beings experience, but if you can make the distinction, and if you keep your symptoms under control, you can seek God (or however you conceive of the sacred), however conceived, with as much vigour as anyone. If you do so, the voice of God doesn't have to be heard in a literal sense.

While this author may have very strong opinions on what sort of spirituality is the best to pursue, the fact of the matter is that having some religious structure of almost any sort can give your life some grounding that it could certainly use. There is nothing about the modern world that has replaced the need for religion, or for spiritual wisdom. The core aching of the human heart is the same as it has always been, and attempting to explain everything in terms of empirical science cannot, in principle, propose any serious answer to the basic questions of "how can I be involved in something greater than myself?" and "what is my purpose?". Philosophy can help a little more, but it's often traditional religions that have more specific answers that are grounded in generations of human experience with the sacred.

Austin's experience of religion has been through a Catholic lens. There are a lot of facets to Catholic faith, but some of the core principles are the importance of forgiveness, both of offenses one has committed and the offenses committed against others, the personal responsibility for one's actions, the redemption of mankind by God's act to save, and the importance of the concept of the Incarnation, where God, the transcendent and infinite being that caused the universe became a human being and took on the finite nature of a human person. We won't explore these ramifications, but one important bit of advice is that if one is trying to discern between different possible religious traditions to keep your focus on the main points, and try not to get lost in the weeds of what, say, a Muslim view of economics is, as interesting as that might be to learn. Major in the majors and minor in the minors, as the saying goes.

A word of warning—if you were raised in a particular religious tradition, it can trick you into thinking you know it better than you actually do. Many people are raised in a faith and pick up bits and pieces, but poor catechesis can lead to a misunderstanding or even outright ignorance of some of the most basic and crucial facts of the religion. It's possible to be raised in a Christian home and not even be able to articulate the basics of the Trinity, or raised Muslim and not even know what its five pillars are. The best place to start is to attempt to see the religion of your upbringing with fresh eyes, and not assume you "get it", because you were in the building (assuming you were). Often, despite the best efforts of parents and the professional religious, you might have just missed it, because your attention was more fixed on things that were more important to you at the time. If you recognize something that you know well, you can move on, but only after you've paid enough attention to confirm that it is what you think it is. Ask questions like "what are the main teachings" and "how does this tradition answer life's biggest questions", and don't take easy, simple answers as good enough.

If you are having trouble discerning the right religious tradition, it's probably best to avoid making it a purely academic exercise. The varying spiritualities that exist are meant to be lived out, not merely contemplated and compared to each other. You have to actually get in there and experience some of what it is like to embody such a religious practice, and you will be missing a lot of pertinent information about how to understand a religion until you go through with practicing it. There may be limits, and you should respect the boundaries that its practitioners put on your participation, but you should be participating in some way to understand the way spirituality operates.

One of the things to consider if you start attending religious gatherings that are unfamiliar to you is that you may have to battle being self-conscious. It's entirely possible to feel out of place and not know what exactly to do, or when to do it, especially when you first start out. First, it's unlikely that people are going to judge you for not blending in. Second, you should look for things the community does to initiate newcomers into the community, because usually these communities want to help you acclimate. Third, just extend yourself the grace of being allowed to be imperfect, as anyone who seems effortless now in doing anything likely put an immense amount of hard work into getting there. You can make the adjustment, don't just give up due to some discomfort at first.

Overall, you just sort of have to get out there and learn something about your religious tradition and possibly others that you are inclined to explore, because the only spirituality that is completely irrational is attempting to not have one. Is there one true religion? Insofar as some religions posit to provide truth, at least there is no more than one. But that may not be the pressing question to you. The move towards religion is a move towards a humanity deepened by the bonds to our ancestors and descendants alike.

Historical and Contemporary Figures

with Schizophrenia

We are going to make a quick change of pace and take a look at a few other notable individuals who lived with schizophrenia. Though Austin Mardon remains the focus of this book and none of the figures mentioned will be explored in anywhere close to the same depth, we felt it was valuable to know about other people who lived with the same condition you or your loved one is now living with.

One of the most notable Schizophrenic figures from history is John Nash. He was brilliant, erratic, inspirational, and had countless accolades he'd collected over the years to go with it. During his early academic years, he displayed the social awkwardness and immaturity that would later become one of his characteristics, but he was a bright student who benefitted much from the extra tutoring offered at home by both of his parents. John Nash was not secluded during his adolescence, despite his social awkwardness, as he was known to have a close network of acquaintances in his neighborhood. John Nash first encountered serious mathematics at the age of 13 when he read E.T. Bell's book, *Men of Mathematics*. As he proceeded to delve further and further into the world of mathematics, those around him began to take note. Teachers and colleagues were impressed by his gift in mathematics, and it led to him being offered a scholarship to Carnegie Institute of Technology after high school. His pathway in university was an interesting one as he found himself jumping from major to major, trying to decide what area he wanted his talent to flourish in. He started off by studying chemical engineering, followed by chemistry, until eventually he arrived at mathematics. His brilliance shone through, and Nash was noticed instantly for his mathematical abilities, with one of his instructors referring to him as a math genius in his Princeton University recommendation. He began his studies in 1948 at Princeton University where he would perform most of his groundbreaking work in mathematics, including the formulation of his Nash Equilibrium and advances to game theory. At Princeton University he began to cement his place in the mathematics world, earning his PhD there for his work on non-cooperative games, which would eventually earn him the Nobel Prize. Up until this point, John Nash was simply a genius mathematician showing no signs of slowing down, and continuing to contribute to our understanding of various concepts. However, the earliest indications of his disease finally appeared around 1958 while he was teaching at Massachusetts Institute of Technology. He would disappear for days on end without warning and return with no explanation, would go off into long reveries in the middle of his lectures, would make seemingly meaningless statements to colleagues and students, and, most importantly, he became increasingly paranoid, not allowing visitors at his office to stand between him and the door and believing that he was being followed at all times. John Nash's psychiatrists came to a quick conclusion and diagnosed him with paranoid schizophrenia based on his intricate system of delusions. He hired a lawyer to petition for his release, and after 50 days in imprisonment and agreeing to outpatient therapy, he was finally able to return home with the help of his wife. His life for the next 20 years or more was marked by periodic hospitalizations interspersed with periods of varying mental and physical health. During this period, he often lived in his own world which, while unusual to others around him, was entirely reasonable and commonplace to himself. Despite his illness, he was able to contribute innovative and excellent work during these times John Nash received several prizes for his work in mathematics during his life – including the famous John Von Neumann Theory Prize in mathematics – but he is arguably best recognized for receiving the Nobel Memorial Prize in Economic Sciences in 1994. Unfortunately, as John Nash and Alicia were taking a cab down the New Jersey Turnpike on May 23rd, 2015, following their visit to Norway - where Nash received the Abel Prize – the driver lost control and crashed. John Nash was 86 years old with a lot left to provide to the world, and his death came as a complete shock to everyone in the mental health industry, as well as those in academics. Despite the untimely end, John Nash lives on as one of the most famous mathematicians in recent centuries.

Another notable figure in the Schizophrenic community was Zelda Sayre. Sayre was born to a renowned middle-class couple with roots in both Montgomery and Confederate history, and was born on July 24th, 1900, in Montgomery. She has been labeled many things during and especially after her life. Many rumors and myths were tied to her name, and yet still we recognize her today for her creative and talented skills in the art of literature – skills that had been often overshadowed during her lifetime. Zelda, named after a gypsy heroine from an 1874 novel, was already a strong presence in Montgomery social circles by her early youth, starring in ballet performances and reveling in the glitter of elite country club dances. Her brazen energy enthralled people around her, and she served as an inspiration for much of the creative work of her husband – F. Scott Fitzgerald. Zelda was crucial to Scott's career, whereas he relentlessly eliminated her contributions and destroyed her autonomy and ability to succeed on her own. Scott had always praised Zelda's writing, but he was quick to point out to her doctor that she lacked his skill. He was enraged by the work's influence on his own long-delayed novel after reading it. Before they got married, Scott was an unpublished author who was amazed by Zelda's personality and wished to marry her. She, however, did not feel the same way, due to him being looked upon by society as a struggling author. Once Scott was able to publish his first book, he was able to finally catch the attention of Zelda and the two became romantically linked, having their first child not long after. Their famously tumultuous marriage was marked by drunkenness, violence, financial ups and downs, and Zelda's mental health struggles, with Zelda spending her life in and out of mental health centers. The Great Depression hit the family hard, leaving them impoverished, and in the end Zelda's marriage to Scott was proved to be a charade. Scott died of a heart attack on December 21, 1940, at the age of 44. Over time Zelda regained her energy and began painting again in her family's mansion during her last few years in Montgomery. Unfortunately, her mental health eventually failed, and she perished tragically in a fire at Highland Hospital in Asheville, North Carolina, on March 10, 1948. She is buried with her husband in the graveyard of the Old St. Mary's Catholic Church in Rockville, Maryland. At the time of her death, she was working on her second unfinished novel, Caesar's Things.

There are also a few historical figures that brought light to Schizophrenia. One of them was Camille Claudel who was diagnosed with schizophrenia when her symptoms became mild. Eventually after her diagnosis she actually began burning her own work due to symptoms of the disorder. Progressing to 1905 and onward she was unable to produce anything fresh during the period she was in hospital. Janet Frame was another historic figure based in New Zealand who was diagnosed with schizophrenia. In New Zealand, she spent eight years in and out of mental facilities. In her late 30s, her schizophrenia diagnosis was overturned. Frame was an author who, after showing signs, was diagnosed officially in 1945 and resulted in her having to stay in Seacliff Mental Hospital after an erratic episode which led to a rather chaotic situation with her to blame. Lastly, and quite possibly the most controversial from the historic figures mentioned today, there is Vincent Van Gogh. Vincent Van Gogh was an artist whose work influenced 20th-century art significantly. Due to his major depression, Vincent Van Gogh was supposedly diagnosed with schizophrenia and epilepsy as well. He recovered in a matter of days after being prescribed medication from the physician and was able to paint Self-Portrait with Bandaged Ear and Pipe, which depicts him in tranquil serenity, around 3 weeks after his admittance.

Clearly not every figure here had as happy as life as one would hope; though not all of their misfortunes were related to their illness, it would be dishonest to pretend that having schizophrenia was ever easy or non-impactful on their lives. I hope that in reading about their hardships though, you do not fail to see all that they still managed to achieve and do while living with their illness. For the most part living in times when having a mental disorder could damn you as a freak or outcast for the remainder of your life, many of these people managed to continue – in the face of abuse and the symptoms of schizophrenia and depression, many continued. Things are not going to be easier now that you are living with schizophrenia, but hopefully this brief change of pace helps show you that, while life will change due to schizophrenia, it doesn't have to end. Even a hundred or more years ago people managed to make it, so if you keep going you can too.

The Path Forward

While the messages of hope and carrying on - and all the reasons that remain to do both - are the main things Austin and us want for you to take away from this book, a close second is just how important it is to find something that you want to do, and which gives you purpose. The two sentiments actually go fairly hand in hand, as though it will be hard early on and throughout your new lives, finding something that gives you a sense of fulfillment in life not only helps with carrying on, it's also kind of one of the main things to be hoping for. There is no one correct way to find fulfillment in your life, and we have actually already covered a number of paths you could take: music, art, religion and/or spirituality, any other hobby of interest - if you enjoy doing them enough, and want to focus your new life on them, there's nothing wrong with that. As we have already touched upon them though, and since this book still largely revolves around telling Austin's story in order to share what he's learned about this life, this chapter is going to focus more so on what Austin directed his new life towards. So, going forward into this chapter, don't feel as though working or volunteering are the only 'correct' or 'valid' paths forward for you. Whatever brings your life meaning and helps you move forward, even if only for a time, is worthwhile and likely just as if not more valid. Take what you can from Austin's experiences, and apply them to your life as it best suits you.

As has been mentioned before, Austin's current life is a pretty far cry from anything he imagined for himself. Though the level of frugality likely would have been similar - if not the same - with or without his schizophrenia, the direction Austin's life took after being diagnosed and the path he ended up walking differed greatly from the life of academia and education he had planned. When he was young, Austin largely planned to follow in his father's footprints of pursuing a doctorate and committing himself to academia. While still an educator of sorts in his current life, offering mentorship and teachings to everyone he works with, Austin ended up dedicating his life to helping others. After sorting out having enough money to survive, Austin was encouraged to go out and volunteer. During his time at the hospital, he felt as though his life were over and that he could no longer contribute anything anymore. With the suggestion of volunteering though, Austin found his way - though small at first - to work and do something with his time.

Austin's options weren't limitless mind you; though he had the strength of will to push on and make an impact, Austin had a number of hurdles to overcome and new realities to adjust to. Due to a combination of the illness and the side effects of the medications for it, Austin found he struggled to do even basic tasks at first. Even as medications moved away from glorified sedatives Austin's "operating parameters" as he put it, had changed. With the help of his mother and father, teaching him how to adjust and the ins and outs of his new life, Austin relearned and widened his parameters - though they wouldn't ever return to how they were before his diagnosis. Though a disheartening note, it is a reality that one has to come to terms with that things aren't going to be the same. Though you are still you, and you are far more than just your illness, no amount of niceties will change the fact that schizophrenia has an impact on you and what you can do. But as is hopefully abundantly clear by now, this is no reason to throw in the towel. There is still a world of things for you to do, more than enough to fill your lifetime and still leave you wishing for more time. So don't get discouraged, because though you will have to learn and adjust, there is plenty of meaning left for you to find.

For Austin, this meaning came from volunteering. Though Austin's work would go on to earn him numerous awards and accolades and help employ hundreds of students with his various books and articles and projects, he started simple. Once he regained some semblance of capacity at everyday tasks, Austin followed the advice he had received and began to volunteer, starting with stuffing envelopes for the Schizophrenia Society in Edmonton. Obviously this is not much compared to what Austin does now, but at the time it was monumental. Austin felt like he could do something again, despite most people telling him to just sit around and drink coffee. He felt useful again. From there, Austin kept at it, giving the first speech on schizophrenia for the Society later that same month. Austin went and found more groups to work with, working with the Prosper Place Clubhouse and Unsung Heroes - two groups committed to helping the mentally ill and providing them with a community. Eventually, Austin even got roped into becoming the leader of Unsung Heroes when the opportunity presented itself and no one stepped up. He used his new position to expand, developing relationships with other nonprofits and the community at large and procuring everyone he could to give speeches and present at Q&A events. Though it started humbly, and was still a ways off of what he does today, what Austin was able to accomplish defied the expectations of everyone around him, and set a precedent for all that can be done if you just keep trying.

As impressive as this all was and still honestly is, more was yet to come. In 1996, Austin had his medication changed to Risperidone, and while it would not become clear to Austin just how great a change it was, it wouldn't be long. The realization of just how much this new medication helped came to Austin when he was trying, yet again, to find his books in the library. Though he had previously been limited by the medications, and as such never succeeded before in his task, this time he found them. While it seems like just another small feat, Austin completed what he had come to believe was an impossible task, and with its completion came renewed confidence in his capabilities. With this restoration and realization, Austin threw himself at another task he once believed was now forever out of his reach: getting a PhD. As can be guessed by the fact that throughout this book Austin has been referred to as Dr. Mardon, he succeeded, and then some, even earning an additional honorary law degree from the University of Alberta years later. As Austin said himself, he could have simply given in, "gone quietly" and given up after being diagnosed. But after a bit of support and an idea (and continuing support along the way), Austin instead chose to rage, against the beliefs and doubt of others, and against the idea that there was nothing left for him now that he was a schizophrenic.

You don't have to pursue academia or chairing volunteer organizations like Austin ended up doing. You don't have to volunteer at all, or go down any road Austin chose to. But what you do have to do is keep going. As dark as it can seem when you're first diagnosed, when you first get put onto meds and branded as 'crazy' by those around you, it's only the end if you let it be. Things suck living with a serious illness. The medications, though improved, still suck - but they let you keep going. Sticking with it, and learning to live with and manage the meds and their various side effects, it lets you function, and gives you control of your life. All you need to do is figure out what you want to do, and there's no better way to do that than trying things and going out there and getting started. Learn the new reality you find yourself in and its limits, come to terms with them, and then do everything you can within them. Hell, maybe even push through and shatter a few more expectations and beliefs held about what you will or won't be able to do now. I mean, Austin was told he'd be dead in a ditch by now - and I've gotta say, he's doing really well for a dead guy. Don't let others' stigmas or ignorance define your life; work to figure out what you can and cannot do yourself.

In no way do I mean to imply that any of that is going to be easy. Not everyone naturally just ignores the doubt and disbelief around them, and a lot of aspects of your new life will make it hard to keep going. But hopefully through the stories, information, and advice presented to you so far in this book - and which will continue to be shared with you through the remainder of it - will help you find a place to start, and help you keep putting one foot in front of the other. Take it slow, don't overwork yourself, listen to your body, and find something to get started with. If you have trouble thinking of what that could be, hopefully the following ideas and resources will help give you some direction.

Finding a volunteering opportunity near you will likely be far easier than you think. At any given time there are countless groups working to help others, both on small and large scales, so anything near you that you are interested in doing would work. And, with the internet as it is, you'll likely be able to quickly find numerous options simply by searching for things near you. In addition to this, there are also likely local schizophrenia or other mental health societies and groups that you could reach out to; though I cannot say with great certainty regarding the United States or other countries, I know in Canada just about every province, if not every province, has a schizophrenia society, as do some cities. For Canada, there's even a national society. Beyond these, there are organizations like Mental Health America (MHA), Schizophrenia and Psychosis Action Alliance, and the National Alliance on Mental Illness (NAMI), all of which offer resources and education, and maybe even volunteer opportunities if you reach out to them for guidance. The truth is though, as I already said, there are any number of opportunities and ways to find volunteering opportunities; odds are, you'll always be able to find a local food bank, or veterans organization, or mental health society or organization. Just find something that you feel good doing, and don't get down if you start something and determine that it isn't right for you. There will always be more opportunities.

A few final notes about moving forward, starting with the fact that there are going to be even more options than listed here. You could find places to help through your local church or religious group, through a school, or you could potentially find simple and manageable work near you that you can handle. And, if you do choose to begin by volunteering, or pursuing a hobby or interest you are passionate about, make sure you sort out finances. This can be confusing and difficult, and I would be lying if I said I knew where to go in every situation. You should be able to work with your healthcare providers to figure out options though, or to get in touch with people who can help.Odds are there are programs and benefits available to help you out if you search for them, things like Assured Income for the Severely Handicapped in Alberta, which Austin got onto back when he was first diagnosed and hospitalized. No matter how uncertain it seems, there are options available to you. You just have to keep searching, and keep fighting. As we move into the final chapter of the book, try and keep in mind what you have taken from Austin's story and our additions to it. Above all else, remember that there is still hope - Austin is an example of all that you can still do if you choose to. So just keep moving forward, and work towards a life that leaves you feeling fulfilled. No matter what others might say, one is still well within your reach.

Day to Day Life

Much like the beginning of the book, we will end the book discussing the day-to-day life of people with schizophrenia. However this time, we won't focus entirely on Dr. Mardon's day, we'll focus on you. This concluding chapter should serve to help you succeed and make progress every day. After all, that's what this book is meant to be about - not just surviving with schizophrenia, but succeeding, no matter what that means to you!

Even though I just said this chapter will focus more on you and not Dr. Mardon, I think he can serve as a great role model. As we said in the first chapter, Austin has a unique life, even without taking the schizophrenia into account, and trying to directly emulate what he does is probably unrealistic. However, what is important to take away from Dr. Mardon's life is that he maintains a routine, stays on top of his medications, and experiences new things every day. Experiencing new things isn't too difficult for Austin, since when you manage hundreds of students throughout a year there are bound to be unique challenges daily, and this is where you and Austin may differ - but the other aspects should serve as an example of what to do.

Having a set routine, as Dr. Mardon does, is very important for a few reasons. First, it helps to ensure you take your meds every day, something that Austin himself would stress the importance of. Second, it helps to make sure you are making proactive decisions that will help you long-term. Austin mentioned in his interview for the first chapter of this book that he had roughly 1000 forms to complete when he applied for veteran's disability. Could you imagine letting that amount of work pile-up to the last minute? That creates a stressful situation as you ruminate on it for weeks, and then an even more stressful period of you rushing to fill out the forms in time. Now, I'm not saying you will ever face a mountain of paperwork quite like this - but tackling necessary things, such as paperwork, proactively is such an excellent way to reduce the amount of stress in your life. Thirdly, having a structured routine can help you to focus less on your illness, and more on your life. If you don't have to spend your whole day reminding yourself about your medications because you took them as part of your schedule, you'll have much more energy to put towards your work, relationships, or hobbies.

What implementing a structured routine like this does for you is immense. In addition to all that I expressed above, it sets you up for success by allowing you to spend more time working on what makes you happy - whether that's a part-time or full-time job, volunteering, exercising, or anything else. But there was another aspect of Dr. Mardon's life that is important for his success, and that is the constant flow of new experiences keeping him from getting bored. We discussed this in the chapters on hobbies and art & music, how keeping yourself from boredom is crucial to reduce onset of symptoms. So, it's important to fill your free time with a hobby or a job, but it's also important to make sure you don't rely entirely on one thing. Consider volunteering a few days a week, and challenging yourself on the other days to try something new - even if it's as small as writing a poem when you usually write in your journal. Even minute things like this are beneficial in opening up your mind to new things and keeping yourself from being bored.

It's also important to keep up and maintain your relationships, both romantic and platonic. It may be starting to sound like there is too much to do in a day, but in an ideal scenario you have time in your day for necessities, hobbies, and relationships. Obviously, life gets complicated and this isn't always possible - but, you can take steps to make managing your relationships easier. For example, you can invite your friends or partner to join you while volunteering, or include them in your hobby. You can also join them in one of their hobbies or activities, and this can both provide you new experiences and contribute to bonding time with your social circle.

In talking about relationships, we discussed some scenarios regarding getting your diagnosis in the middle of a relationship, at the start, or before you even begin. This can be an awkward scenario but part of coming to terms with your diagnosis is revealing yourself to others - of course, this should be done at your own pace and comfort. But, perhaps more importantly, the idea of working through problems together was discussed thoroughly. This is something that everyone deals with, mental illness or not, and managing problems together is crucial to the success of the relationship - but we use the word manage for a reason. All you can do is work together to come to the best solution to the problem, even if it's imperfect, because no relationship is ever perfect. It's the couples who know how to communicate and compromise who make it, and this is not dissimilar to managing your schizophrenia. In the same way that you need to be open to treatment and support for your schizophrenia, you need to be open to conversation and compromise in your relationship.

Platonic relationships (that is, friendships) are equally as important to your well-being as romantic ones, and they fulfil different aspects of life. A solid social circle helps you to get through some of the worst parts of your illness, by engaging you in a social activity, or simply just being someone to talk to. The same is true for your friends - you are somebody that they can rely on when they need you, and that kind of connection can be powerful in improving your self-image and well-being. In our chapter on these types of relationships, we discussed how to manage losing friendships, making new friends, and strengthening your current relationships. What it all boils down to is openness and honesty. Your friends can't help you if you're not honest with them, and when they try to help, you need to be open. Besides, as we discussed, trying new things is a healthy way to keep busy, and who better to try new things with than your friends! Finally, there's one more key point in platonic relationships that is important to remember, and that is sometimes just having fun for the sake of having fun. Not everything has to be specifically about trying to just 'make it' with schizophrenia - in fact, it's healthy to try and forget about it sometimes and just enjoy things for the sake of it, and it will still end up contributing to positive progress in your life.

Religion and spirituality, whatever they mean to you, are powerful feelings that can help you through the toughest times of your life. Now, there is reason to be cautious in this field, especially among those with schizophrenia, as voices and visions can often be religious in nature. But that doesn't mean you should just disregard religion entirely. As was mentioned in our chapter on this topic, nothing makes a religious voice better or worse than a normal voice in your head, and it shouldn't dissuade you from doing some soul-searching. After you get your diagnosis may actually be when you're most inspired to seek spirituality - this is quite a common reaction. And, like many other aspects of life, openness is key. Even those who grew up in religious households shouldn't assume they know everything about that religion, and should explore it and others.

In practicing religion & spirituality, the structure of an organized religion can provide many benefits in what may be otherwise untouched areas of your life. First and foremost, a church, temple, mosque, or otherwise can be a safe haven for you, and the religious leaders there can offer support. But spirituality provides benefits in your everyday life too, as we discussed in the chapter - the main one being gratitude. Researching and practicing a religion can vastly improve your sense of gratitude for all the good in your life. This contributes overall to the improvement of your self-image and outlook on life - perhaps two of the most critical parts of success.

It's impossible to draw a framework for day-to-day life that works for everyone. What works for Dr. Mardon may not work for you, and vice versa. There is no one size fits all solution for almost anything in life, let alone as challenging a diagnosis of schizophrenia. The most important takeaway from this book is utilizing a host of different strategies to fulfill your life, and achieve success, whatever that means to you. By applying the aspects of all these chapters to your life, you can find that success. Of course, it may not be easy, and not much in life is - but taking the first step is the most important part. Going to the volunteer center, or the church, or the social event you're nervous about is the important first step on your path to living a successful life. Hopefully, at the very least, the book opened you up to some new ideas on how to manage and move forward while dealing with schizophrenia, and gave you the knowledge and confidence to take that first step.

Resources

https://www.mhanational.org/conditions/schizophrenia Mental Health America

https://schizophrenia.ca/about/ Schizophrenia Society of Canada

https://sczaction.org/ Schizophrenia and Psychosis Action Alliance

https://nami.org/Home National Alliance on Mental Illness

https://www.alberta.ca/aish.aspx Assured Income for the Severely Handicapped (AISH)

https://www.ncbi.nlm.nih.gov/pmc/articles/PMC5999799/ Holistic Management of Schizophrenia Symptoms Using Pharmacological and Non-pharmacological Treatment - from US National Library of Medicine

https://www.ncbi.nlm.nih.gov/pmc/articles/PMC6386427/ Exercise as a Treatment for Schizophrenia: A Review - from US National Library of Medicine

https://www.mtabc.com/what-is-music-therapy/how-does-music-therapy-work/mental-health/ Music Therapy Association of British Columbia

https://eric.ed.gov/?id=EJ777009 Role Development Applied to Art Therapy Treatment of an Artist Diagnosed with Schizophrenia - Victoria P. Schindler, Pomona, NJ, and Carol Pletnick - 2006 - accessed via MacEwan Library

www.ingramcontent.com/pod-product-compliance
Lightning Source LLC
Chambersburg PA
CBHW030853270326
41928CB00008B/1357